5

D1107918

PUNCH AND JUDY

Written and Illustrated by

PETER FRASER

Accompanied by the dialogue
of the puppet show

B. T. Batsford Limited, London
Van Nostrand Reinhold Company
New York VNR

Filmset in Great Britain by Filmtype Services Limited,
Scarborough, Yorkshire
Printed and bound in Great Britain
for the publishers
B. T. Batsford Limited, 4 Fitzhardinge Street, London W.1
and
Van Nostrand Reinhold Company, 450 West 33rd Street,
New York, N.Y. 10001

CONTENTS

INTRODUCTION

In order to do a Punch and Judy Show successfully, it is important to know a little of its background history. It will then be seen why the show came to be performed in a certain way and from there it can be judged what may well be brought up to date, and what should remain unchanged.

MR PUNCH

Many people think of the Punch and Judy Show as part of Victorian England and certainly, as a street show, it belonged mainly to that period. Punch himself, however, is much older. Before the Victorian era began he was well known in England as a string puppet called Punchinello, a noisy knock-about character with a shrill artificial voice and a very coarse sense of humour. He was so popular in the eighteenth century that he appeared (sometimes quite unreasonably) in half the puppet plays of the time, both in the fashionable marionette theatres of London, and in fairground shows throughout the country.

Mr Punch first came to England from France to join in the celebrations following the Restoration in 1662. He can be traced from France back to Italy at the end of the sixteenth century, where he is recognized as a masked live actor with a great nose who performed in the impromptu Italian Comedy at Naples. His character and appearance have been added to over all these years. In this country Punch has adopted the red and yellow costume of the English clown, and some of the habits of the traditional Court Jester and rustic comedians of folk drama going back to the Middle Ages. Today we still enjoy his delightful irreverence in dealing with conventional beliefs and attitudes. He does just what he likes and gets away with it!

THE PUNCH AND JUDY SHOW

Although Punch himself came from abroad, much of the story and many of the characters of the Punch and Judy Show are British. At the end of the eighteenth century fashionable interest moved from the marionette theatre to the live stage, and puppet showmen had to take to the London streets to make a living. The new audience was found among simple people, familiar mostly with fairground entertainment and themes still surviving from early folk drama. Punch joined himself to the traditions they knew and developed a drama of his own, full of vigorous action and impromptu humour to attact the passers by, but echoing the mystery plays and mummers plays of centuries before.

The way in which the Punch and Judy Show is presented shows the effect of performing to an audience with little money, and of constant movement from street to street in search of fresh spectators. Glove puppets and a booth were used because they were light in weight, easily moveable, and could be seen over the heads of the crowd. The drama developed as a succession of incidents which the audience could join or leave at any time, and much of the show was impromptu, being lengthened or shortened according to prospects of payment. The showman avoided the expense of other manipulators by working the puppets himself, one on each hand. For this reason only two puppets could appear together, Punch remaining firmly on the showman's right hand, with the left hand changing puppets below the opening of the booth as each new character appeared in turn. Only one assistant was necessary—to blow a trumpet (later he played pan-pipes and beat a drum), collect money from the crowd, and help carry the booth from pitch to pitch.

6

The glove puppet may well be called the traditional English puppet, as it has been used continuously in England from Elizabethan times, perhaps from an even earlier date. At periods when marionettes from Italy have gained a more fashionable popularity, the glove puppet has still survived in fairgrounds and in the streets, as it still does today in the Punch and Judy Show.

Glove puppets are worked from below in a booth open at the top in front, and follow the movements of the hand and finger of the operator. Usually in this country the index finger fits into the head of the puppet, and the thumb and middle fingers fit inside its arms. Some showmen add the fourth to the third finger in the puppets right arm. This method of operation is not symmetrical in appearance, but the thumb and index finger are most useful in gripping and holding. Apart from striking, throwing, holding and head nodding the individual movements of glove puppets are limited, but they are rapid and decisive being closely linked to the movements of the operator's hand and arm. This directness of control makes the glove puppet particularly suitable for strong characterisation as there is no barrier between operator and puppet. The speech and action of the manipulator are easily carried out together, and the puppet's performance is a direct projection of the performance of the showman himself. These qualities of the glove puppet are part of the reason for the success and durability of the Punch and Judy Show. No other puppet could so successfully carry out the vigorous action and impromptu haranguing of the audience which give it such vitality.

THE TEXT OF THE PLAY

In the past, in England, puppet plays have been handed down from one generation of showmen to another mainly by word of mouth. Very few Punch and Judy Shows have been written down and much of the value of the performance has always belonged to its impromptu nature. With each new generation dialogue and music have tended to mirror events, personalities, and popular songs of the time.

It is surprising then to find that after 200 years, and in spite of variations in the performances of successive showmen in the streets and more recently at the seaside, the drama of Punch and Judy remains the same. Punch continues to fight his wife and the law, the hangman and the devil. He continues to treat marriage, authority, death, and the fear of eternity with the same disrespect. A few characters from the earlier performances have been replaced, but the important characters concerned with these themes remain. Where they do not the reason is usually found in the wish to make the play more suitable for children. When this arises from the attitude that puppets are for children only I think this is a pity.

The following script was first published in 1828 and is an account of one of the best and possibly the earliest of the Punch and Judy Shows which appeared in the London streets towards the end of the eighteenth century. It belonged to an Italian showman called Piccini who, in his old age, gave a special performance from which a book was written by John Payne Collier, and illustrated by George Cruikshank. This script should be compared with another printed in 1856 in volume III of Henry Mayhew's *London Labour and the London Poor* and with any others of more recent date which can be found. I have chosen to use the earliest because, in spite of some unnecessary re-arrangements by its editor, I do not feel that later versions have improved upon it. I have also based my puppets and their costumes on the Cruikshank drawings. But it is probably not desirable to give an exact performance of *any* script unless as a scholarly exercise. Today, as it always has in the past, the Punch and Judy Show should reflect some of the personality of its showman, and cast a satirical eye at current events, attitudes, and celebrities.

We have seen how for economic reasons the drama of Punch and Judy became a one man show. In schools and colleges however the same limitations do not apply, and the project may be extended to cover a large group. As long as Punch remains constant to one manipulator, the rest of the cast may be divided among fourteen or more, and, space allowing, more than two characters may appear at once.

In this book I have given details of different ways of making glove puppets to suit various grades of skill. In the past, professional Punch and Judy figures have always been made of wood to stand up to hard knocks, constant usage, and outdoor weather. Where durability is less important, papier mâché construction will do very well, and brings the making of puppets within the scope of a much wider group. Where puppetry is used for educational aims, the flexibility of the Punch and Judy drama and cast is of great value; and in psychiatric work with children the basic situations of family and authority offer many opportunities for identification.

THE CHARACTERS
OF THE DRAMA

The following puppets are taken from the book of the 1828 Punch and Judy performance. This show presented thirteen human characters and two animals, a larger cast than is usually found today. Punch, Judy, Toby, the Baby, the Doctor, the Constable, Jack Ketch and the Devil are seen in nearly every Punch and Judy show, while others have been dropped or replaced. Three new puppets, Joey a Clown, the Ghost of Judy and a Crocodile are fairly common in later versions.

In name and costume both Punch and Scaramouch suggest their Italian origin, but several others are recognisable English types of their period, perhaps carved from life. In making Punch and Judy puppets today you may choose to present characters in modern dress. Although there is less variety and colour in today's costume than in the early nineteenth century, the Punch and Judy show does stay alive by reflecting life around it.

PROPORTIONS

These puppets are limited in height by the length of the performers' fingers, hand and forearm, and have special proportions of their own. In human beings the head as a unit of measurement is not more than one-seventh of the total height. By this rule a glove puppet 460 mm would have a head only 65 mm high and features barely visible to the audience! For this reason the heads of glove puppets are made much larger in proportion to their bodies than is found in real life, and are usually a quarter or one-fifth of the total height.

MR PUNCH

The basic appearance of Mr Punch seldom varies. He has a large hooked nose meeting a long chin, a humped back and an elaborate red and yellow costume with a ruff at the neck. Mr Punch is usually shown carrying a stick, and his hat, known as a 'sugar loaf', has a tassel hanging forward in front. His personality, easily understood on reading the script of the play, shows an honest admission of every human failing! To this may be added some of the personality of the showman himself.

13

SCARAMOUCH AND TOBY

The name Scaramouch is better known as a trick puppet in the marionette theatre than in the Punch and Judy show. He is Toby's master in this version but is not seen again. I have presented Toby as a glove puppet, but many people prefer to remember Toby as a live dog wearing a ruff and sitting on the playboard to take his part.

JUDY AND THE BABY

Judy nearly always wears a mob cap and apron. In early Punch and Judy shows she was full of fight and spirit; but recently she has become more long-suffering, making a second appearance in the show as a ghost. There are many ways of representing the baby, but I think the most successful ones bear some likeness to Punch the father.

PRETTY POLLY

Punch's girl friend only appears in the early version of the Punch and Judy show, which is a pity as she does suggest a reason for Judy's behaviour. She is not a glove puppet (which can have no waist line) but a doll on a stick.

THE DOCTOR AND THE COURTIER

The Doctor is seen in nearly every Punch and Judy show. Today he might appear in a white coat with a stethoscope. The Courtier has no part in the story of Punch and Judy at all, but was used as a trick puppet who could remove his hat with one hand and stretch and turn his neck to display the skill of the showman.

HECTOR

Hector the horse is most easily made flat from plywood or hard-board painted on both sides. A real mane, harness and tail give an effect of three dimensions, and this is all that is needed as long as he is seen from side view only. In an up-to-date version of Punch and Judy, Hector could be changed to a motor-car!

THE BLIND MAN AND THE SERVANT

The blind man looks like a rogue which is just as well if we are to
sympathise with Punch's treatment of him. He has been dropped
from later Punch and Judy shows. The servant is the earliest of a
long tradition of negroes, becoming a great favourite in the middle
of the 1800s as Jim Crow.

THE CONSTABLE AND THE OFFICER

These are the two characters representing the law in the early
Punch and Judy show, and may also be used in the coffin carrying
scene. The three cornered hat of the constable remained in use
for the beadle of later shows; and when the police force came
into being, the officer became a policeman with a helmet.

JACK KETCH THE HANGMAN AND THE DEVIL

Both of these characters appear in every Punch and Judy show.
The hanging of Jack Ketch by trickery has always been popular,
and no audience will forgive the showman if Punch does not beat
the Devil. Sometimes Jack Ketch is dressed in a skull cap and
black mask. The Devil may be in black or red; black contrasting
well with Punch's coat in the final scene.

DRAMATIS PERSONÆ

Mr Punch
The Dog Toby
Scaramouch
Judy
The Child
Pretty Polly
A Courtier
Hector the Horse

The Doctor
A Servant
A Blind Man
A Constable
An Officer
Jack Ketch
The Devil

THE TRAGICAL COMEDY, OR THE COMICAL TRAGEDY OF PUNCH AND JUDY

Enter PUNCH—*After a few preliminary squeaks, he bows three times to the spectators; once in the centre, and once at each side of the stage, and then speaks the following*

PROLOGUE

Ladies and Gentlemen, pray how you do?
If you all happy, me all happy too.
Stop and hear my merry littel play;
If me make you laugh, me need not make you pay.

Exit

ACT I   SCENE I

PUNCH *is heard behind the scene, squeaking the tune of* Malbroug
s'en vat en guerre; *he then makes his appearance and dances
about the stage, while he sings to the same air.*

> Mr Punch is one jolly good fellow,
> His dress is all scarlet and yellow,
> And if now and then he gets mellow,
> > It's only among his good friends.
> > His money most freely he spends;
> > To laugh and grow fat he intends;
> With the girls he's a rogue and a rover;
> He lives, while he can, upon clover;
> When he dies—it's only all over;
> > And there Punch's comedy ends.

He continues to dance and sing, and then calls 'Judy, my dear!
Judy!'

Enter THE DOG TOBY

PUNCH Hollo, Toby! who call'd you? How you do, Mr Toby?
Hope you very well, Mr Toby.
TOBY Bow, wow, wow!
PUNCH How do my good friend, your master, Mr Toby? How
do Mr Scaramouch?
TOBY Bow, wow, wow!
PUNCH I'm glad to hear it. Poor Toby! What a nice good-
tempered dog it is! No wonder his master is so fond of him.
TOBY (*snarls*) Arr! Arr!
PUNCH What! Toby! you cross this morning? You get out of
bed the wrong way upwards?
TOBY (*snarls again*) Arr! Arr!
PUNCH Poor Toby. (*Putting his hand out cautiously, and trying
to coax the dog, who snaps at it*) Toby, you're one nasty cross dog:
get away with you! (*strikes at him*)
TOBY Bow, wow, wow! (*Seizing* PUNCH *by the nose*)
PUNCH Oh dear! Oh dear! My nose! my poor nose! my beauti-

ful nose! Get away! get away, you nasty dog—I tell your master. Oh dear! dear!—Judy! Judy!

Punch *shakes his nose, but cannot shake off the Dog, who follows him as he retreats round the stage. He continues to call* 'Judy! Judy, my dear!' *until the Dog quits its hold and exit*

PUNCH (*solus, and rubbing his nose with both hands*) Oh my nose! my pretty littel nose! Judy! Judy! You nasty, nasty, brute, I will tell your master of you. Mr Scaramouch! (*calls*) My good friend, Mr Scaramouch! Look what you nasty brute dog has done!

SCENE II

Enter SCARAMOUCH *with a stick*

SCARAMOUCH Hollo! Mr Punch! What have you been doing to my poor dog?

PUNCH (*retreating behind the side scene, on observing the stick, and peeping round the corner*) Ha! my good friend! how you do? glad to see you look so well. (*aside*) I wish you were farther with your nasty great stick.

SCARAMOUCH You have been beating and ill-using my poor dog, Mr Punch.

PUNCH He has been biting and ill-using my poor nose.—What have you got there, sir?

SCARAMOUCH Where?

PUNCH In your hand?

SCARAMOUCH A fiddle.

PUNCH A fiddel! what a pretty thing is a fiddel!—can you play upon that fiddel?

SCARAMOUCH Come here, and I'll try.

PUNCH No, thank you—I can hear the music here, very well.

SCARAMOUCH Then you shall try yourself. Can you play?

PUNCH (*coming in*) I do not know, 'till I try. Let me see! (*takes the stick, and moves slowly about, singing the tune of the* 'Marche de

Marselloise'. *He hits* Scaramouch *a slight blow on his high cap, as if by accident*)

SCARAMOUCH   You play very well, Mr Punch. Now, let me try. I will give you a lesson how to play the fiddle. (*takes the stick, and dances to the same tune, hitting Punch a hard blow on the back of his head*) There's sweet music for you.

PUNCH   I no like you playing so well as my own. Let me again. (*takes the stick, and dances as before: in the course of his dance he gets behind* Scaramouch, *and, with a violent blow, knocks his head clean off his shoulders*) How you like that tune, my good friend? That sweet music, or sour music, eh? He! he! he! (*laughing, and throwing away the stick*) You'll never hear such another tune, so long as you live, my boy. (*sings the tune of* 'Malbroug', *and dances to it*) Judy, my dear! Judy! can't you answer, my dear?

JUDY   (*within*) Well! what do you want, Mr Punch?

PUNCH   Come upstairs: I want you.

JUDY   Then want must be your master. I'm busy.

PUNCH   (*singing tune* 'Malbroug').

    Her answer genteel is and civil!

No wonder, you think, if we live ill,
And I wish her sometimes at the Devil,
　　Since that's all the answer I get.
　　Yet, why should I grumble and fret,
　　Because she's sometimes in a pet?
Though I really am sorry to say, Sirs,
That that is too often her way, Sirs.
For this, by and by, she shall pay, Sirs.
　　Oh, wives are an obstinate set.

Judy, my dear! (*calling*) Judy, my love! pretty Judy! come up stairs.

SCENE III

Enter JUDY

JUDY　Well, here I am! what do you want, now I'm come?
PUNCH　(*aside*) What a pretty creature! An't she one beauty?
JUDY　What do you want, I say?
PUNCH　A kiss! a pretty kiss! (*kisses her, while she hits him a slap on the face*)
JUDY　Take that then: how do you like my kisses? Will you have another?
PUNCH　No; one at a time, one at a time, my sweet pretty wife. (*aside*) She always is so playful.—Where's the child? Fetch me the child, Judy, my dear.

Exit JUDY

PUNCH　(*solus*) There's one wife for you! What a precious darling creature? She go to fetch our child.

Re-enter JUDY *with the* CHILD

JUDY　Here's the child. Pretty dear! It knows it's papa. Take the child.
PUNCH　(*holding out his hands*) Give it me—pretty littel thing!

28

How like its sweet mamma!
JUDY   How awkward you are!
PUNCH   Give it me: I know how to nurse it so well as you do.
(*she gives it him*) Get away!

Exit JUDY

PUNCH   (*nursing the child in his arms*) What a pretty baby it is!
was it sleepy then? Hush-a-by, by, by.—(*sings to the tune of* Rest
thee, babe)

> Oh, rest thee, my baby,
>   Thy daddy is here:
> Thy mammy's a gaby,
>   And that's very clear.
> Oh rest thee, my darling,
>   Thy mother will come,
> With voice like a starling;—
>   I wish she was dumb!

Poor dear littel thing! it cannot get to sleep: by, by; by, by, hush-a-by. Well, then, it shan't. (*dances the child, and then sets it on his lap, between his knees, and sings the common nursery ditty*)

> Dance baby diddy;
> What shall daddy do widdy?
>   Sit on his lap,
>   Give it some pap;
> Dance baby diddy.

(*After nursing it upon his lap,* PUNCH *sticks the child against the side of the stage, on the platform, and going himself to the opposite side, runs up to it, clapping his hands, and crying,* 'Catchee, catchee, catchee!' *He then takes it up again, and it begins to cry*)

What is the matter with it. Poor thing! It has got the stomach ache, I dare say. (*child cries*) Hush-a-by, hush-a-by! (*sitting down and rolling it on his knees*) Naughty child!—Judy! (*calling*) the

child has got the stomach ache. Pheu! Nasty child! Judy. I say!
(*child continues to cry*) Keep quiet, can't you? (*hits it a box on the
ear*) Oh you filthy child! What have you done? I won't keep such
a nasty child. Hold your tongue! (*strikes the child's head several
times against the side of the stage*) There!—there!—there! How
you like that? I thought I stop your squalling. Get along with you,
nasty, naughty, crying child. (*throws it over the front of the stage
among the spectators*)—He! he! he! (*laughing and singing to the
same tune as before*)

> Get away, nasty baby;
> There it goes over:
> Thy mammy's a gaby,
> Thy daddy's a rover.

Re-enter JUDY

JUDY Where is the child?

PUNCH Gone,—gone to sleep.

JUDY What have you done with the child, I say?

PUNCH Gone to sleep, I say.

JUDY What have you done with it?

PUNCH What have I done with it?

JUDY Ay; done with it! I heard it crying just now. Where is it?

PUNCH How should I know?

JUDY I heard you make the pretty darling cry.

PUNCH I dropped it out at window.

JUDY Oh you cruel horrid wretch, to drop the pretty baby out at window. Oh! (*cries and wipes her eyes with the corner of her white apron*) You barbarous man. Oh!

PUNCH You shall have one other soon, Judy, my dear. More where that come from.

JUDY I'll make you pay for this, depend upon it.

Exit in haste

PUNCH There she goes. What a piece of work about nothing! (*dances about and sings, beating time with his head, as he turns round, on the front of the stage*)

Re-enter JUDY *with a stick. She comes in behind, and hits* PUNCH *a sounding blow on the back of the head, before he is aware.*

JUDY I'll teach you to drop my child out at window.

PUNCH So-o-oftly, Judy, so-o-oftly! (*rubbing the back of his head with his hand*) Don't be a fool now. What you at?

JUDY What! you'll drop my poor baby out at window again, will you? (*hitting him continually on the head*)

PUNCH No, I never will again. (*she still hits him*) Softly, I say, softly. A joke's a joke!

JUDY Oh you nasty cruel brute! (*hitting him again*) I'll teach you.

PUNCH But me no like such teaching. What! you're in earnest, are you?

JUDY Yes, (*hit*) I (*hit*) am (*hit*)

PUNCH I'm glad of it: me no like such jokes. (*she hits him again*) Leave off, I say. What! you won't, won't you?

JUDY No, I won't. (*hits him*)

PUNCH Very well: then now come my turn to teach you. (*He*

32

snatches at, and struggles with her for · 'e stick, which he wrenches from her, and strikes her with it on the · ·d, while she runs about to different parts of the stage to get out o{ ·us way) How you like my teaching, Judy, my pretty dear? (*hitting her*)

JUDY   Oh pray, Mr Punch. No more!

PUNCH   Yes, one littel more lesson. (*hits her again*) There, there, there! (*she falls down with her head over the platform of the stage; and as he continues to hit her, she puts up her hand to guard her head*) Any more?

JUDY   No, no, no more! (*lifting up her head*)

PUNCH   (*knocking down her head*) I thought I should soon make you quiet.

JUDY   (*again raising her head*) No.

PUNCH   (*again knocking her down, and following up his blows until she is lifeless*) Now if you're satisfied, I am. (*perceiving that she does not move*) There, get up Judy, my dear; I won't hit you any more. None of your sham-Abram. This is only your fun. You got the head-ache? Why, you only asleep. Get up, I say.—Well, then, get down. (*tosses the body down with the end of his stick*) He, he, he! (*laughing*) To lose a wife is to get a fortune. (*sings*)

> 'Who'd be plagued with a wife
>   That could get himself free
> With a rope or a knife,
>   Or a good stick, like me.'

SCENE   IV

Enter PRETTY POLLY

PUNCH   (*Seeing her, and singing out of* The Beggar's Opera *while she dances*)

> When the heart of a man is oppress'd with cares,
> The clouds are dispelled when a woman appears, etc.

PUNCH   (*aside*) What a beauty! What a pretty creature! (*extend-*

33

*ing his arms, and then clasping his hands in admiration. She continues
to dance, and dances round him, while he surveys her in silent delight.
He then begins to sing a slow tune and foots it with her; and, as the
music quickens, they jig it backwards and forwards, and sideways, to
all parts of the stage. At last,* PUNCH *catches the lady in his arms
and kisses her most audibly, while she appears 'nothing loth'. After
waltzing, they dance to the tune of* 'The White Cockade', *and*
PUNCH *sings as follows:*)

> I love you so, I love you so,
> I never will leave you; no, no, no:
> If I had all the wives of wise King Sol,
> I would kill them all for my Pretty Pol.

Exeunt dancing

ACT II   SCENE I

Enter a FIGURE *dressed like a courtier, who sings a slow air, and moves to it with great gravity and solemnity. He first takes off his hat on the right of the theatre, and then on the left, and carries it in his hand. He then stops in the centre; the music ceases, and suddenly his throat begins to elongate, and his head gradually rises until his neck is taller than all the rest of his body. After pausing for some time, the head sinks again; and, as soon as it has descended to its natural place, the* FIGURE *exits*

SCENE II

Enter PUNCH *from behind the curtain, where he had been watching the manoeuvres of the* FIGURE

PUNCH Who the devil are you, me should like to know, with your long neck? You may get it stretched for you one of these days, by somebody else. It's a very fine day. (*peeping out, and looking up at the sky*) I'll go fetch my horse, and take a ride to visit my pretty Poll. (*he sings to the tune of* Sally in our Alley)

> Of all the girls that are so smart,
>   There's none like pretty Polly:
> She is the darling of my heart,
>   She is so plump and jolly.

Exit singing

Re-enter PUNCH *leading his* HORSE *by the bridle over his arm. It prances about and seems very unruly.*

PUNCH Wo, ho! my fine fellow, Wo, ho! Hector. Stand still, can't you, and let me get my foot up to the stirrup.

(*while* **Punch** *is trying to mount, the horse runs away round the stage, and* PUNCH *sets off after him, catches him by the tail, and so stops him.* PUNCH *then mounts, by sitting on the front of the stage, and with both hands lifting one of his legs over the animal's back. At first, it goes pretty steadily, but soon quickens its pace; while* PUNCH, *who does not keep his seat very well, cries,* 'Wo, ho! Hector, wo, ho!' *but to no purpose, for the* HORSE *sets off at full gallop, jerking* PUNCH *at every stride with great violence.* PUNCH *lays hold round the neck, but is ultimately thrown upon the platform*)

PUNCH   Oh, dear! Oh, Lord! Help! Help! I am murdered! I'm a dead man! Will nobody save my life? Doctor! Doctor! Come, and bring me to life again. I'm a dead man. Doctor! Doctor! Doctor!

SCENE III

DOCTOR   Who calls so loud?
PUNCH   Oh, dear! Oh, Lord! Murder!
DOCTOR   What is the matter? Bless me, who is this? My good friend, Mr Punch? Have you had an accident, or are you only taking a nap on the grass after dinner?
PUNCH   Oh, Doctor! Doctor! I have been thrown; I have been killed.
DOCTOR   No, no, Mr Punch; not so bad as that, sir: you are not killed.
PUNCH   Not killed, but speechless. Oh, Doctor! Doctor!
DOCTOR   Where are you hurt? Is it here? (*touching his head*)
PUNCH   No; lower.
DOCTOR   Here? (*touching his breast*)
PUNCH   No; lower, lower.
DOCTOR   Here then? (*going downwards*)
PUNCH   No; lower still.
DOCTOR   Then, is your handsome leg broken?

PUNCH   No; higher. (*as the* DOCTOR *leans over Punch's legs, to examine them,* PUNCH *kicks him in the eye*)
DOCTOR   Oh, my eye! my eye!

Exit

PUNCH   (*solus*) Aye, you're right enough: it is my eye, and Betty Martin too. (*jumping up and dancing and singing, tune* Malbroug)

> The Doctor is surely an ass, sirs,
> To think I'm as brittle as glass, sirs;
> But I only fell down on the grass, sirs,
>   And my hurt—it is all my eye.

(*while* PUNCH *is singing and dancing, the* DOCTOR *enters behind, and hits* PUNCH *several times on the head.* PUNCH *shakes his ears*)

PUNCH   Hollo! hollo! Doctor, what game you up to now? Have done! What you got there?
DOCTOR   Physic, Mr Punch. (*hits him*) Physic for your hurt.
PUNCH   Me no like physic: it give me one headache.
DOCTOR   That's because you do not take enough of it. (*hits him*

38

again) The more you take, the more good it will do you. (*hits him*)
PUNCH   So you Doctors always say. Try how you like it yourself.
DOCTOR   We never take our own physic, if we can help it. (*hits him*) A little more, Mr Punch, and you will soon be well. (*hits him*)

(*During this part of the dialogue, the* DOCTOR *hunts* PUNCH *to different parts of the stage, and at last gets him into a corner, and belabours him until* PUNCH *seems almost stunned*)

PUNCH   Oh, Doctor! Doctor! no more, no more! Enough physic for me! I am quite well now.
DOCTOR   Only another dose. (*hits him*)
PUNCH   No more!—Turn and turn about is all fair, you know. (PUNCH *makes a desperate effort, closes with the* DOCTOR, *and after a struggle succeeds in getting the stick from him*) Now, Doctor, your turn to be physicked. (*beating the* DOCTOR)
DOCTOR   Hold, Mr Punch! I don't want any physic, my good sir.
PUNCH   Oh, yes, you do; you very bad: you must take it. I the Doctor now. (*hits him*) How do you like physic? (*hits*) It will do you good. (*hits*) This will soon cure you. (*hits*) Physic! (*hits*)

39

Physic! (*hits*) Physic. (*hits*)

DOCTOR   Oh, pray, Mr Punch, no more! One pill of that physic is a dose.

PUNCH   Doctors always die when they take their own physic. (*hits him*) Another small dose, and you never want physic again. (*hits him*) There; don't you feel the physic in your inside? (PUNCH *thrusts the end of the stick into the* DOCTOR'*s stomach: the* DOCTOR *falls down dead, and* PUNCH, *as before, tosses away the body with the end of his staff*) He, he, he! (*laughing*) Now Doctor, you may cure yourself, if you can.

(*Sings and dances to the tune of* Green grow the rushes, O)

> Right toll de riddle doll,
> There's an end of him, by goll!
>   I'll dance and sing,
>   Like anything,
> With music for my pretty Poll.

Exit

SCENE IV

Enter PUNCH, *with a large sheep-bell, which he rings violently, and dances about the stage, shaking the bell and his head at the same time, and accompanying the music with his voice; tune* Morgiana in Ireland.

> Mr Punch is a very gay man,
> He is the fellow the ladies for winning oh;
> Let them do whatever they can,
> They never can stand his talking and grinning oh.

Enter A SERVANT, *in a foreign livery.*

SERVANT   Mr Punch, my master, he say he no like dat noise.

PUNCH   (*with surprise and mocking him*) Your master, he say he no like dat noise! What noise?

SERVANT Dat nasty noise.

PUNCH Do you call music a noise?

SERVANT My master he no lika de music, Mr Punch, so he'll have no more noise near his house.

PUNCH He don't, don't he? Very well. (PUNCH *runs about the stage ringing his bell as loudly as he can*)

SERVANT Get away, I say wid dat nasty bell.

PUNCH What bell?

SERVANT That bell. (*striking it with his hand*)

PUNCH That's a good one. Do you call this a bell? (*patting it*) It is an organ.

SERVANT I say it is a bell, a nasty bell.

PUNCH I say it is an organ. (*striking him with it*) What you say it is now?

SERVANT An organ, Mr Punch.

PUNCH An organ? I say it is a fiddle. Can't you see? (*offers to strike him again*)

SERVANT It is a fiddle.

PUNCH I say it is a drum.

SERVANT It is a drum, Mr Punch.

PUNCH   I say it is a trumpet.
SERVANT   Well, so it is a trumpet. But bell, organ, fiddel, drum, or trumpet, my master he say he no lika de music.
PUNCH   Then bell, organ, fiddel, drum, or trumpet, Mr Punch he say your master is a fool.
SERVANT   And he say, too, he will not have it near his house.
PUNCH   He's a fool, I say, not to like my sweet music. Tell him so: be off. (*hits him with the bell*) Get along. (*driving the servant round the stage, backwards, and striking him often with the bell*) Be off, be off. (*knocking him off the stage. Exit* SERVANT. PUNCH *continues to ring the bell as loudly as before, while he sings and dances*)

Re-enter SERVANT, *slily with a stick.*

(PUNCH, *perceiving him, retreats behind the side curtain, and remains upon the watch. The* SERVANT *does the same, but leaves the end of the stick visible.* PUNCH *again comes forward, sets down his bell very gently, and creeps across the stage, marking his steps with his hands upon the platform, to ascertain whereabouts his enemy is. He then returns to his bell, takes it up, and, going quietly over the stage, hits the* SERVANT *a heavy blow through the curtain, and exit, ringing his bell, on the opposite side*)

SERVANT   You one nasty, noisy, impudent blackguard. Me catch you yet. (*hides again as before*)

(*Enter* PUNCH, *and strikes him as before with the bell. The* SERVANT *pops out, and aims a blow, but not quickly enough to hit* PUNCH, *who exit*)

SERVANT   You dirty scoundrel, rascal, thief, vagabond, blackguard, and liar, you shall pay for this, depend upon it.

(*he stands back. Enter* PUNCH *with his bell, who, seeing the servant with his stick, retreats instantly, and returns, also armed with a bludgeon, which he does not at first show. The* SERVANT *comes forward, and strikes* PUNCH *on the head so hard a blow, that it seems to confuse him*)

42

SERVANT   Me teach you how to ring you nasty noisy bell near de gentil-men's houses.

PUNCH   (*recovering*) Two can play at that. (*hits the servant with his stick. A conflict:—after a long struggle, during which the combatants exchange staves, and perform various manoeuvres, PUNCH gains the victory, and knocks his antagonist down on the platform, by repeated blows on the head*)

SERVANT   Oh dear! Oh, my head!

PUNCH   And oh, your tail, too. (*hitting him there*) How do you like that, and that, and that? (*hitting him each time*) Do you like that music better than the other?—This is my bell, (*hits*) this my organ, (*hits*) this my fiddel, (*hits*) this my drum, (*hits*) and this my trumpet, (*hits*) there! a whole concert for you.

SERVANT   No more! me dead.

PUNCH   Quite dead?

SERVANT   Yes, quite.

PUNCH   Then there's the last for luck. (*hits him and kills him. He then takes hold of the body by its legs, swings it round two or three times, and throws it away*)

ACT III   SCENE I

Enter an OLD BLIND MAN, *feeling his way with a staff. He goes to the opposite side, where he knocks.*

BLIND MAN   Poor blind man, Mr Punch. I hope you'll bestow your charity. I hear that you are very good and kind to the poor, Mr Punch. Pray have pity upon me, and may you never know the loss of your tender eyes! (*listens, putting his ear to the side, and hearing nobody coming knocks again*) I lost my sight by the sands in Egypt, poor blind man. Pray, Mr Punch, have compassion upon the poor stone blind. (*coughs and spits over the side*) Only a halfpenny to buy something for my bad cough. Only one half-penny. (*knocks again*)

Enter PUNCH, *and receives one of the knocks, intended for the door, upon his head.*

PUNCH Hollo! you old blind blackguard, can't you see?
BLIND MAN No, Mr Punch. Pray, sir, bestow your charity upon a poor blind man, with a bad cough. (*coughs*)
PUNCH Get along, get along; don't trouble me:—nothing for you.
BLIND MAN Only a halfpenny! Oh, dear! my cough is so bad! (*coughs, and spits in* PUNCH'S *face*)
PUNCH Hollo! Was my face the dirtiest place you could find to spit in? Get away! you nasty old blackguard! Get away! (*seizes the* BLIND MAN'S *staff, and knocks him off the stage; and then begins to sing, in the mock Italian style, the following words, pretending to play the fiddle on his arm, with the stick*)

> When I think on you, my jewel,
>   Wonder not my heart is sad;
> You're so fair, and yet so cruel,
>   You're enough to drive me mad.

44

On thy lover take some pity:
And relieve his bitter smart.
Think you Heaven has made you pretty,
But to break your lover's heart?

SCENE II

Enter A CONSTABLE

CONSTABLE   Leave off your singing, Mr Punch, for I'm come to make you sing on the wrong side of your mouth.
PUNCH   Why, who the devil are you?
CONSTABLE   Don't you know me?
PUNCH   No, and don't want to know you.
CONSTABLE   Oh, but you must: I am the constable.
PUNCH   And who sent for you?
CONSTABLE   I'm sent for you.
PUNCH   I don't want constable. I can settle my own business without constable, I thank you. I don't want constable.
CONSTABLE   But the constable wants you.
PUNCH   The devil he does! What for, pray?
CONSTABLE   You killed Mr Scaramouch. You knocked his head off his shoulders.
PUNCH   What's that to you? If you stay here much longer, I'll serve you the same.
CONSTABLE   Don't tell me. You have committed murder, and I've a warrant for you.
PUNCH   And I've a warrant for you. (PUNCH *knocks him down, and dances and sings about the stage to the tune of* Green grow the rushes, O)

Enter AN OFFICER, *in a cocked hat with a cockade, and a long pigtail.*

OFFICER   Stop your noise, my fine fellow.

45

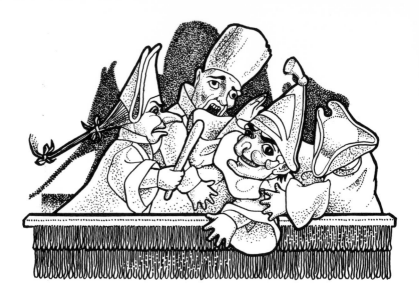

PUNCH   Shan't.

OFFICER   I'm an officer.

PUNCH   Very well. Did I say you were not?

OFFICER   You must go with me. You killed your wife and child.

PUNCH   They were my own, I suppose; and I had a right to do what I liked with them.

OFFICER   We shall see that, I'm come to take you up.

PUNCH   And I'm come to take you down. (PUNCH *knocks him down, and sings and dances as before*)

Enter JACK KETCH, *in a fur-cap.* PUNCH, *while dancing, runs up against him without seeing him.*

PUNCH   (*with some symptoms of alarm*) My dear Sir,—I beg you one thousand pardon: very sorry.

JACK KETCH   Aye, you'll be sorry enough before I've done

with you. Don't you know me?

PUNCH   Oh, sir, I know you very well, and I hope you very well, and Mrs Ketch very well.

JACK KETCH   Mr Punch, you're a very bad man. Why did you kill the Doctor?

PUNCH   In self defence.

JACK KETCH   That won't do.

PUNCH   He wanted to kill me.

JACK KETCH   How?

PUNCH   With his d——d physic.

JACK KETCH   That's all gammon. You must come to prison: my name's Ketch.

PUNCH   *Ketch* that then. (PUNCH *knocks down* JACK KETCH, *and continues to dance and sing*)

Enter behind, one after the other, the CONSTABLE, *the* OFFICER, *and* JACK KETCH. *They fall upon* PUNCH *in the order in which they enter, and, after a noisy struggle, they pin him in a corner, and finally carry him off, while he lustily calls out, Help! murder!' etc.*

SCENE III

The curtain at the back of the stage rises, and discovers PUNCH *in prison, rubbing his nose against the bars and poking it through them.*

PUNCH   Oh dear! Oh dear! what will become of poor pill-garlic now. My pretty Poll, when shall I see you again? (*sings to the air of* Water parted from the sea)

> Punch, when parted from his dear,
>   Still must sing in doleful tune.
> I wish I had those rascals here,
>   I'd settle all their hashes soon!

47

Enter JACK KETCH. *He fixes a gibbet on the platform of the stage, and exit*

PUNCH   Well, I declare now, that very pretty! That must be a gardener. What a handsome tree he has planted just opposite the window, for a prospect!

Enter the CONSTABLE. *He places a ladder against the gibbet, and exit*

PUNCH   Stop thief! Stop thief! There's one pretty rascal for you. He come back again and get up the ladder to steal the fruit out of the tree.

Enter two men with a coffin. They set it down on the platform, and exeunt

PUNCH   What that for, I wonder? Oh dear, I see now: what one fool I was! That is a large basket for the fruit be put into.

JACK KETCH   Now, Mr Punch, you may come out, if you like it.

PUNCH   Thank you, kindly; but me very well where I am. This very nice place, and pretty prospect.

JACK KETCH   What, won't you come out, and have a good dinner for nothing?

PUNCH   Much obliged, Mr Ketch, but I have had my dinner for nothing already.

JACK KETCH   Then a good supper?

PUNCH   I never eat suppers: they are not wholesome.

JACK KETCH   But you must come out. Come out and be hanged.

PUNCH   You would not be so cruel.

JACK KETCH   Why were you so cruel as to commit so many murders?

PUNCH   But that's no reason why you should be cruel, too, and murder me.

JACK KETCH   Come, directly.

PUNCH   I can't; I got one bone in my leg.

JACK KETCH   And you've got one bone in your neck, but that shall be soon broken.—Then I must fetch you. (*he goes to the prison, and after a struggle, in which* PUNCH *calls out, 'Mercy! mercy! I'll never do so again!'* JACK KETCH *brings him out to the front of the stage*)

PUNCH   Oh dear! Oh dear! He quiet—can't you let me be?

JACK KETCH   Now, Mr Punch, no more delay. Put your head through this loop.

PUNCH   Through there? What for?

JACK KETCH   Aye, through there.

PUNCH   What for? I don't know how.

JACK KETCH   It is very easy: only put your head through here.

PUNCH   What, so? (*poking his head on one side of the noose*)

JACK KETCH   No, no, here!

PUNCH   So, then? (*poking his head on the other side*)

JACK KETCH   No so, you fool.

PUNCH   Mind, how you call fool: try if you can do it yourself. Only shew me how, and I do it directly.

JACK KETCH   Very well; I will. There, you see my head, and

you see this loop: put it in, so. (*putting his head through the noose*)
PUNCH   And pull it tight, so! (*he pulls the body forcibly down,
and hangs* JACK KETCH) Huzza! huzza!

(PUNCH *takes down the corpse, and places it in the coffin: he then
stands back. Enter two, who remove the gibbet, and placing the
coffin upon it, dance with it on their shoulders grotesquely, and
exeunt*)

PUNCH   There they go. They think they have got Mr Punch
safe enough. (*sings*)

> They're out! they're out! I've done the trick!
>   Jack Ketch is dead—I'm free;
> I do not care, now, if old Nick
>   Himself should come for me.

Exit

SCENE IV

Enter PUNCH *with a stick. He dances about, beating time on the front of the stage, and singing to the tune of* Green grow the rushes, O.

> Right foll de riddle loll
> I'm the boy to do 'em all.
>   Here's a stick
>   To thump Old Nick,
> If he by chance upon me call.

Enter the DEVIL. *He just peeps in at the corner of the stage, and exit*

PUNCH (*much frightened, and retreating as far as he can*) Oh dear! Oh Lord! Talk of the Devil, and he pop up his horns. There the old gentleman is, sure enough. (*a pause and dead silence, while* PUNCH *continues to gaze at the spot where the* DEVIL *appeared. The* DEVIL *comes forward*) Good, kind, Mr Devil, I never did you any harm, but all the good in my power.—There, don't come any nearer. How you do, Sir? (*collecting courage*) I hope you, and all your respectable family well? Much obliged for this visit—Good morning—should be sorry to keep you, for I know you have a great deal of business when you come to London. (*the* DEVIL *advances*) Oh dear! What will become of me? (*the* DEVIL *darts at* PUNCH, *who escapes, and aims a blow at his enemy: the* DEVIL *eludes it, as well as many others, laying his head on the platform, and slipping it rapidly backwards and forwards, so that* PUNCH, *instead of striking him, only repeatedly hits the boards*)

Exit DEVIL

PUNCH He, he, he! (*laughing*) He's off: he knew which side his bread buttered on. He one deep, cunning devil. (PUNCH *is alarmed by hearing a strange supernatural whirring noise, something like the rapid motion of fifty spinning-wheels, and again retreats to the corner, fearfully awaiting the event*)

Re-enter the DEVIL, *with a stick. He makes up to* PUNCH, *who retreats round the back of the stage, and they stand eyeing one another and fencing at opposite sides. At last, the* DEVIL *makes a blow at* PUNCH, *which tells on the back of his head*

PUNCH   Oh, my head! What is that for? Pray, Mr Devil, let us be friends. (*the* DEVIL *hits him again, and* PUNCH *begins to take it in dudgeon, and to grow angry*) Why, you must be one very stupid Devil not to know your best friend when you see him. (*the* DEVIL *hits him again*) Be quiet! I say, you hurt me!—Well, if you won't, we must try which is the best man—Punch or the Devil.

(*here commences a terrific combat between the* DEVIL *and* PUNCH: *in the beginning, the latter has much the worst of it, being hit by his black adversary when and where he pleases; at last, the* DEVIL *seems to grow weary, and* PUNCH *succeeds in planting several heavy blows. The balance being restored, the fight is kept up for some time, and towards the conclusion* PUNCH *has the decided advantage, and drives his enemy before him. The* DEVIL *is stunned by repeated blows on the head and horns, and*

52

falls forward on the platform, where PUNCH *completes his victory, and knocks the breath out of his body.* PUNCH *then puts his staff up the* DEVIL's *black clothes, and whirls him round in the air, exclaiming:*) Huzza! huzza! the Devil's dead!

CURTAIN

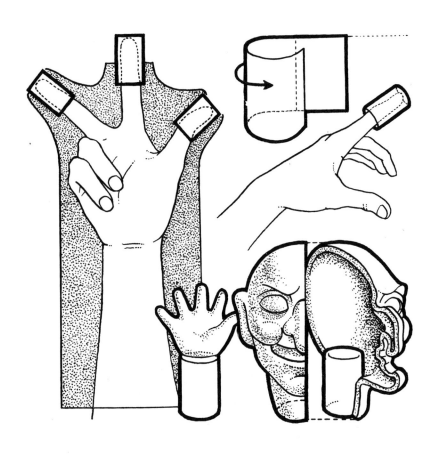

INSIDE THE GLOVE PUPPET

The mechanism of the glove puppet is based on three cylinders which fit comfortably on to the thumb, index and middle finger. These cylinders are attached to the head and two hands of the puppet, and are glued into the sleeves and neck of the puppet's body. This principle remains the same in all glove puppets although in wood carving the hollow wrist and hand may be carved in one.

Usually the three cylinders are made of cardboard which is rolled round each finger and thumb for measurement and glued. The card should reach the second joint of each of the fingers, and the first joint of the thumb. The cylinders can be padded inside with thin foam rubber sheet for comfort.

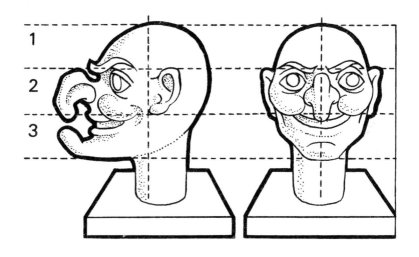

1

2

3

PROPORTIONS OF THE HEAD

MAKING THE HEAD

There are four commonly used methods of making puppet heads.

1 Direct modelling in papier mâché over a plasticine base.
2 Lining a plaster of paris mould made from a plasticine base.
3 Direct modelling in papier mâché over a permanent core.
4 Carving in wood.

For the first two methods, and also as a guide for carving in wood, a plasticine model is first made. When constructing a head from imagination it is useful to have some knowledge of its average proportions. The facing diagram shows how even the grotesque head of Punch himself follows a basic plan, with the nose lying in the centre third of three horizontal divisions. Seen from the side, the ear also lies in this space which is measured from the browline to the tip of the nose.

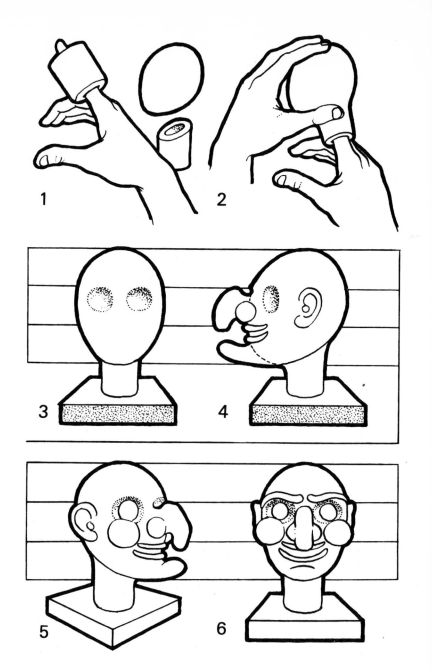

The facing drawings show how a plasticine head can be built up in simple stages on a 80 mm high peg stand. The neck is measured by rolling a ribbon of plasticine round the top half of the index finger; the head is an egg shape 102 mm high. Eye sockets are pressed out with the thumb, and features are built on to this basic shape by fingers and modelling tool.

When a group of people are making heads for Punch and Judy characters, they should decide together on a uniform size of head. A good average height for a glove puppet head is 102 mm, although Punch himself may be rather larger because of his importance.

MAKING A PLASTICINE MODEL

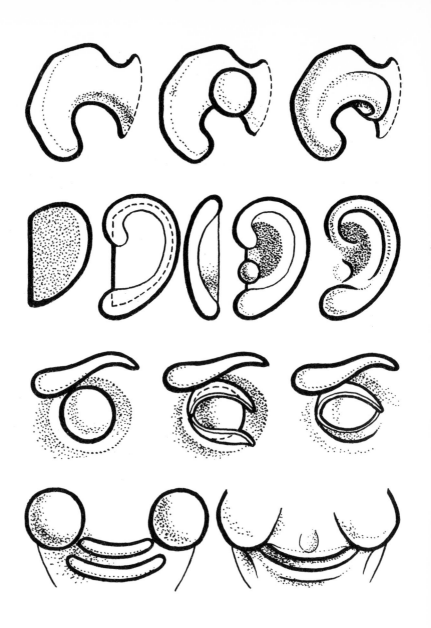

BUILDING UP FEATURES

Although professional Punch and Judy puppets are usually carved in wood, there are many traditional ways of making puppets in papier mâché. Properly prepared, this under-rated medium is excellent for direct modelling or for lining plaster of paris moulds. Recently there have appeared on the market one or two modelling substances which set permanently hard. These require no preparation but usually have to be baked or boiled, and tend to be expensive. In either case methods of modelling and casting are similar.

There are two types of papier mâché, laminated and pulped, which may be combined or used separately. Preparation of papier mâché takes time, but a group working together can quickly make enough for several puppets.

Laminated papier mâché is built up in layers. Sugar paper, or paper handkerchiefs for fine work, are more easily shaped than newspaper. The sheets are soaked in stationers gum or liquid size, and squeezed out ready to be laid in place. As work progresses the paper is torn into pieces small enough to fit the prepared core or greased mould to be covered. The first layer is put on without paste. Several further layers are pasted on both sides with flour paste or cold water paste. The final layer is pressed smooth with a wetted finger.

Papier mâché pulp is made from newspaper or paper towelling torn into pieces as small as 6 mm square. Four double sheets of newspaper or a similar amount of paper towelling are enough for a puppet's head and hands. The torn paper is soaked in water overnight, thoroughly sifted and rubbed while still in the basin, then removed and squeezed dry. Into this bulk of paper fibre, $\frac{1}{4}$ parts of modelling clay and of ceiling whiting are kneaded. Finally paste is added until the pulp can be rolled between the fingers without crumbling.

Work dries quickly if placed near a radiator or in an oven, but papier mâché should be removed from moulds while still flexible enough to be loosened from undercuts without damage. Both types of papier mâché must be smoothed when dry. They may be wet sand-papered or coated with wood grain filter. The finished surface is sealed with spirit varnish, and may be painted with oil, poster, or acrylic paint.

DIRECT MODELLING OVER A PLASTICINE BASE

In this method of puppet-head making, a plasticine base is covered with laminated papier mâché. When the covering is nearly dry it is cut in half, removed from the plasticine core, and re-assembled as a light hollow head.

Torn paper handkerchiefs follow a simple contour very well. The model is painted with a thin coat of vaseline which holds the first layer of paper in place. A further four or five layers are pasted over each other, and a wooden modelling tool helps to smooth and define the details.

If the covering is cut from the model before it is quite dry, the two halves can be fitted together while still flexible. Working through the hole in the base of the neck, the halves are attached on the inside with bandage and paste, and the whole inside surface can be strengthened in the same way.

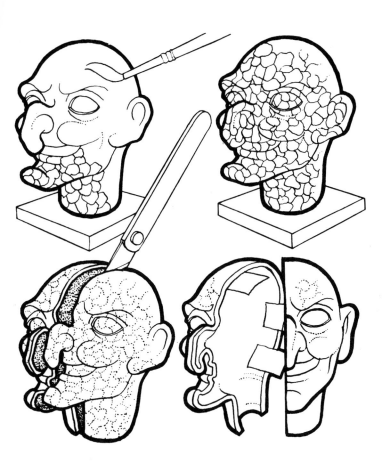

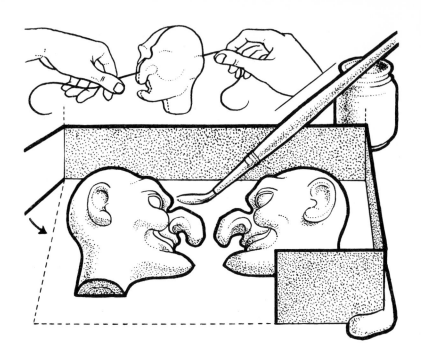

MAKING A PLASTER MOULD

There are several ways of making plaster of Paris moulds. The following box method is the most easily controlled.

1   A plasticine model of the head is cut in two with a length of thin wire. To avoid the undercuts of Punch's nose and chin this cut is made from the front to the back of the head.

2   The two halves are laid flat side down, 13 mm apart on a smooth surface—this may be a sheet of zinc or plastic. A cardboard wall, 13 mm higher than the parts of the head, is placed round the two halves, sealed at the joints with plasticine, and tied round with tape.

3   The surface within the box frame surrounding the two halves is painted with vaseline to allow easy removal of the finished mould.

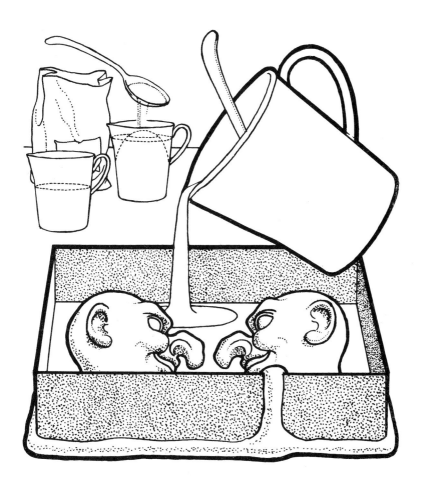

4   Pour enough water into a large jug to fill the space inside the cardboard surround, and to cover the halves of the head by 13 mm.

5   Plaster of Paris powder is shaken rapidly into the water until the sediment shows above the surface. The powder and water are sifted and stirred until smooth and creamy, and in a few minutes the mixture begins to thicken.

6   The liquid plaster is now poured in one continuous flow into the box space, and the board or sheet underneath is shaken to release air bubbles. The plaster soon begins to harden and becomes quite warm in the process.

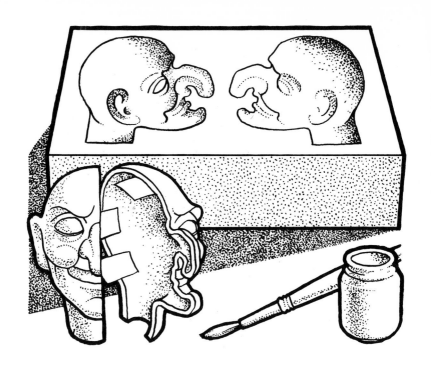

7 After fifteen minutes the cardboard surround may be peeled away and the hardened mould prized off its greased base. The two halves of the plasticine head are picked out and the inside surface sponged clean with soap and water. The mould can be lined with papier mâché, plastic wood, or any hardsetting modelling substance. Before papier mâché is used the mould is greased with vaseline; for plastic wood it must be soaked first in water.

Laminated papier mâché can be built in several layers of different coloured paper. This makes certain that each layer is completed before the next begins. Papier mâché pulp is laid in pellets which are pressed together into a skin fitting close against the shape of the mould. This pressure is repeated during drying to prevent distortion through shrinkage. Other plastic linings are usually laid into the mould in one piece like pastry into a dish and pressed into shape.

The linings are prised out when nearly dry and glued together with paper or cloth hinges inside.

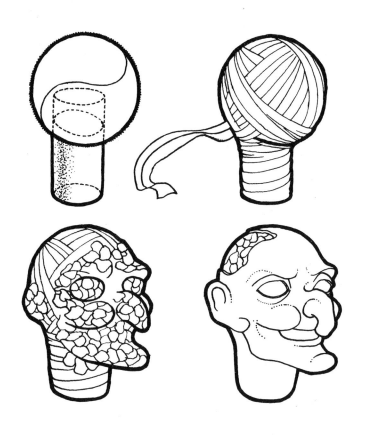

DIRECT MODELLING OVER A PERMANENT CORE

This is the most immediately expressive way of making puppet heads, and is very suitable for work with children.

A tennis ball pierced by a cardboard tube makes a good permanent base for the head and neck. The cardboard tube is rolled round the index finger for measurement, and is glued into a hole cut in the ball. Both ball and tube are then bound with torn rag or with bandage, which provides an absorbent base for the papier mâché.

Plenty of paste should be used between the bandaging and the first of the layers of laminated papier mâché which form the basic shape of the features. When this coat is partly dry, finer modelling in papier mâché pulp completes the head. Papier mâché pulp is shaped by pinching and pressing rather than by a building up method. When the pulp layer is half dry, a further pressure over the whole surface prevents shrinkage and cracking.

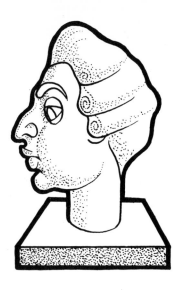

CARVING A HEAD IN WOOD

Unless you are an experienced woodcarver, it is always safest to begin by making a plasticine model of the head to be carved. Then, when you start to carve, you will know exactly the shapes you are aiming for. Carving in wood takes skill and intelligence. A carver must be able to see basic forms under detail, and resist the temptation to start finer cutting before the simpler stages are completed. For those who have not the aptitude for handling woodcarving tools, it is wiser to stick to papier mâché construction which is more directly expressive. Balsa wood, which might be considered easy to work, is disappointing as any instrument but a razor blade tends to crush rather than to cut it.

For the sake of clearness I have used the head of the Doctor not of Punch, for these drawings. Punch's nose creates problems which are dealt with later. The stages of cutting also are more defined in diagram than in practice where the process is continuous and overlapping.

Choice of wood The detailed carving of a puppet's head and hands demands a wood that is hard and close grained. All fruit woods have this quality, but limewood is by far the most easily cut and has a waxy texture which does not easily splinter. Many Punch

and Judy puppets in the past have been carved from ash. Wood bought from a timber yard should be well seasoned and ready to work.

Tools A full set of wood carver's tools is seldom found nowadays and without skilled training cannot be used effectively. For most purposes of carving I find that a 25 mm firmer chisel and a 10 mm chisel for finer work do very well if kept properly sharpened. Those who carve frequently will add in time their own set of narrower chisels and gouges where they find a special use for them. Other tools that you will need are a mallet, file, small needle file, and sandpaper where a smooth surface is asked for; also a saw or plane to shape the wood into a rectangle before carving.

It is very important that work should be kept firmly in position during carving, and held without damage to cutting already done. In early stages a vice or G clamp may be used. If the carving of the ears is left until last, the head can be held in place with pressure at those points. In later stages a block of wood may be screwed as a temporary fixture to the base of the head being carved. This block itself can be held in a vice. I usually complete the carving holding the wood in a cloth in one hand, while the other hand files or hand pares with a small chisel.

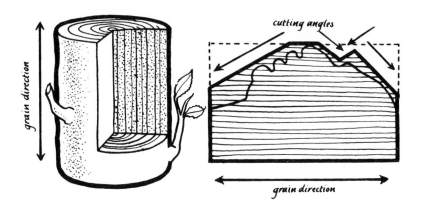

Wood grain An understanding of the grain direction of wood is essential if you are going to carve successfully. A cross section of naturally growing wood shows yearly divisions of growth expanding in rings from the centre. A vertical section shows the lines of grain direction caused by these rings. Chisel cuts must always be made at an angle moving in the same direction as the grain. If this principle is forgotten essential parts of the carving will split along the grain lines. In a glove puppet the grain direction is most easily followed when it runs from the crown to the chin in the head, and from the wrists to fingertips of the hands.

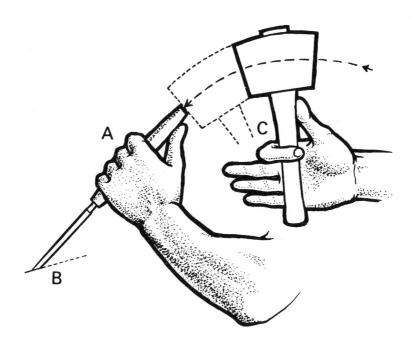

Using a mallet and chisel The mallet strikes the handle of the chisel in a series of sharp taps, rather than with great blows which would dislodge the wood from the vice. In this way there is more control over the chisel's direction which may be adjusted between each stroke.

A   The chisel is held lightly between the fingers and thumb of the left hand and is not gripped hard in the fist.

B   For most purposes of carving, the cutting angle of the chisel lies against the wood. Where the flat surface of the chisel is in contact, the cutting direction tends to curve into the work.

C   The mallet, like the chisel, is lightly held. The main support comes from the index finger and thumb which also act as a pivot, the three lower fingers working as a trigger. This arc of movement is usually sufficient for fine carving. Movement from the shoulder or elbow is seldom necessary.

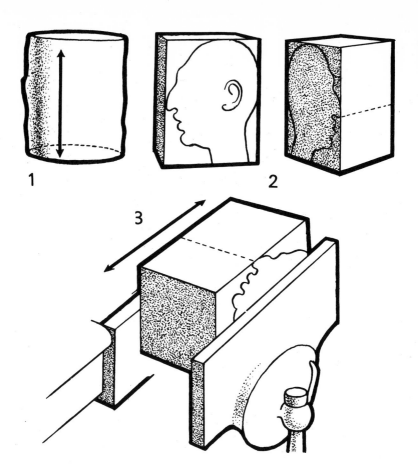

Carving

1　The wood you are going to cut may be circular or rectangular in section. In either case it must be reduced by planing to a rectangular block just over the height and width of your plasticine model. The grain direction runs from the top of the head to the neck.

2　The side profile of the head is drawn on each side of the block and the point of the nose, the most prominent part of the face, is marked in a line across the front.

3　The block is now placed face upwards in the vice ready for cutting to begin.

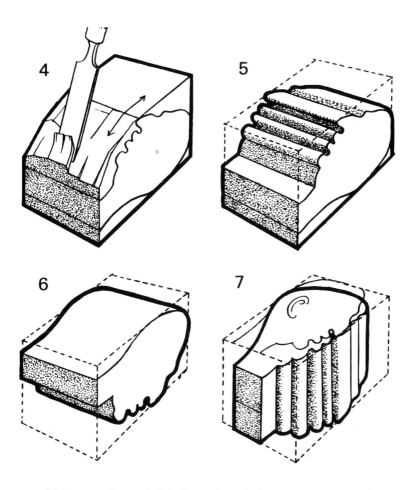

4 Using a mallet and chisel, two broad planes are now cut; the surface areas from the nose to the neck, and from the nose to the top of the head.

5 All the angles of the features in profile are chiselled out, the direction of cutting altering where necessary to follow the grain.

6 The head is now reversed in the vice, and the profile of the back of the head is cut.

7 The head is turned sideways in the vice and padded with folded rag to protect the nose. The sides of the head are cleared in each direction from the ears.

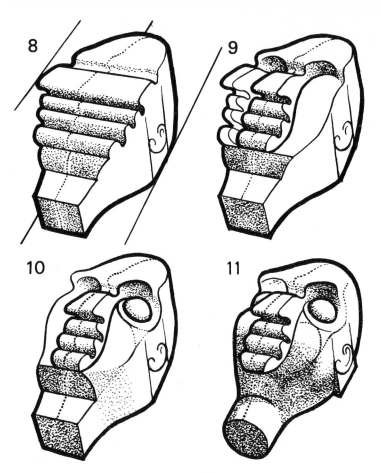

8 The head is turned face upwards and held in the vice by the ears. The eyebrows and the centre line of the face are marked in pencil.

9 Two deep cuts, starting from the brows, define the width of the nose, mouth and chin. The whole face is lowered on either side of these features.

10 Carefully watching grain direction, a groove is cut round each eye socket, and the rounding of the cheeks is begun.

11 The whole head is rounded back and front. This may be done in the vice with a chisel, or the head can be removed and filed.

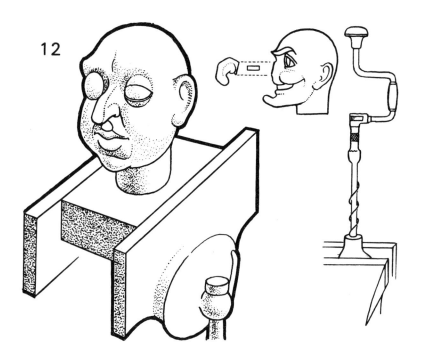

12　From this stage onwards the head can be held in the hand, or screwed from beneath to a block held in the vice. Details of features are now completed, and you may aim at a smooth finish or leave the natural texture of the chisel marks. Much of the character will depend on added paint and hair.

Experienced wood carvers sometimes prefer to cut the hair in wood as part of the whole head. When making Punch himself it may be necessary to carve the nose separately, as the wood available does not always allow room for nose and head in one.

When carving is completed, the neck shaft is bored with a brace and size 20 mm bit. To prevent damage to features the head must be wrapped in a cloth in the vice while this is done. Some wooden heads are very heavy, but if the crown of the head is sawn off, much of the inside may be cleared out with a gouge. When the top is replaced the join is concealed by hair.

Before you colour papier mâché or wood, the surface must be prepared to prevent the paint from sinking in. A coat of spirit varnish after glass-papering seals papier mâché, and wood can be finished with grainfilled powder and water rubbed in with the finger. Other modelling substances can usually be painted without preparation.

Oil paint and acrylic paint are both waterproof and are suitable for most surfaces. Oil paint has a translucent quality which is good for faces and hands; acrylic paint has a flatter appearance but can be thinned with water and is very quick drying.

The painting of puppets' faces should bring out character and expression, and sometimes the faces of Punch and Judy puppets are painted with the crude but lively make-up of the circus clown. You may prefer a more natural colouring, but a strong outline round the eyes helps them to be seen at a distance. I find scarlet outline for male puppets, and blue for Judy and Polly very effective, with a touch of varnish on the pupil to catch the light.

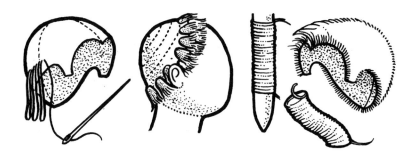

HAIR

Hair can be made as part of the modelling or carving of the head. Where it is added later you may use real hair, dolls' hair, fur or wool. Sometimes a skull cap is made of stiff material into which wool or dolls' hair can be sewn. Fur or lamb's wool can be cut and stretched to the same pattern. When hair is glued directly to the head it is wisest to do it in small overlapping hanks. Curls can be made by wrapping wool round a greased knitting needle, painting it with thin gum, and sliding off when dry.

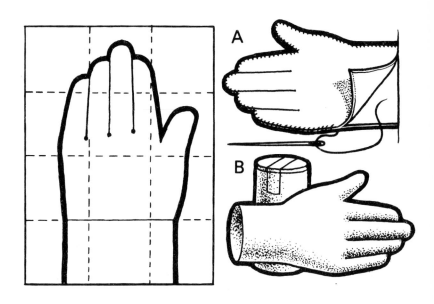

MAKING HANDS

The hands of a glove puppet are almost as important as its face in expressing character. Different puppets will have different types of hands; long and narrow, short and square, open or close-fingered. There are several ways of making hands, and each method is suitable for a particular type. The size of hands is a matter of choice. I prefer to make them $\frac{1}{5}$th of the total height of the puppet, in proportion to the body rather than to the head.

FELT HANDS

The pattern opposite shows an average shape for a felt hand. The extra length beyond the wrist slides over the cardboard cylinder which fits on to the operator's thumb or third finger. Two pieces (*A*) are cut for each hand, and stitched together round the edge by oversewing. The whole hand is then turned inside out and stuffed with flock or cotton wool, a knitting needle being useful in turning and shaping the thumb. Finger divisions are stitched in last through the stuffing, and the cardboard cylinder is closed at the wrist end (*B*) before the felt hand is glued into place. Felt hands are easy to make but can only be designed with closed fingers.

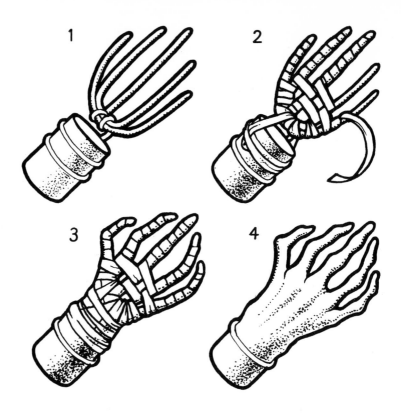

PAPIER MÂCHÉ HANDS

This method of papier mâché construction is very suitable for open-fingered irregular positions of the hand.

1   Two curved pieces of wire roughly 102 mm long, are bound together by a third which forms both the middle finger and an attachment to the cardboard cylinder.

2   Strips of rag or roller bandage build up the bulk of the hand and wrist.

3   Fingers may now be bent into any shape or position suited to the character or action of your puppet.

4   The fabric surface is soaked with paste, and covered by a layer of papier mâché pulp pressed into shape.

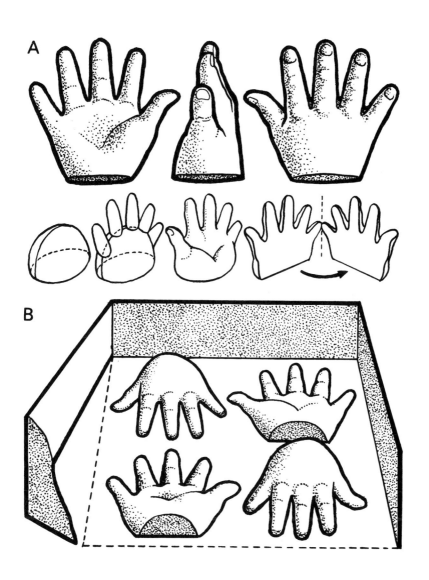

MAKING PLASTICINE HANDS FOR A PLASTER MOULD

Hands can be cast from a plaster of Paris mould using the same method described in the making of puppet heads. When several puppets are made together this saves time. Two hands are first modelled in plasticine. (*A*) They must be of a shape (short and thick) that can be easily divided. The four halves are laid 102 mm apart in a cardboard surround to make a one piece mould. (*B*)

The completed mould may be lined with papier mâché pulp, plastic wood or any hard setting modelling substance. (*C*) Hands, being small, are usually made solid. If papier mâché is used, it is safer to add a core of thin wire (*D*) when the two halves are sealed together. When each hand is glued in position on the end of its cardboard tube, the joint is strengthened with a strip of tape round the wrist. (*E*)

C

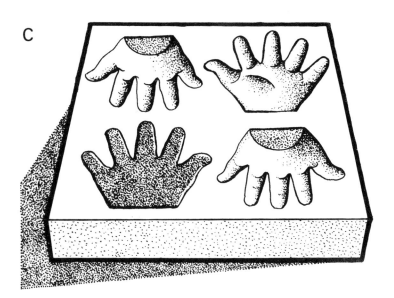

D

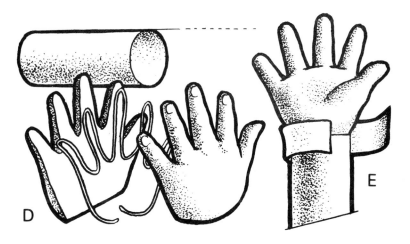

E

85

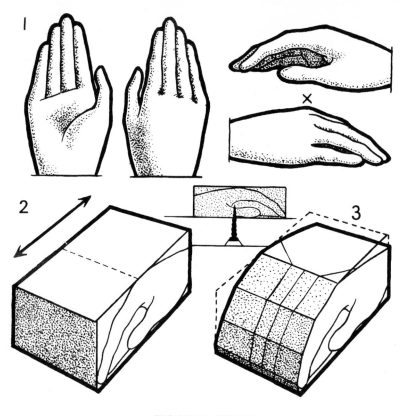

WOODEN HANDS

If you have successfully carved a puppet's head in wood you will find the planning and cutting of hands very similar.

1   A plasticine model shows the basic form of the hand. This is the best position for a beginner to attempt, with the palm hollowed and the knuckle of the index finger at the highest point.

2   A block of close-grained wood is marked with the side profile of the hand, and a line across the top marks the knuckles. The grain direction runs from wrist to finger-tip.

3   The hand is held in position on a block of wood in the vice by means of a screw through the palm. The top of the hand is cleared in either direction from the centre, and the positions of index and middle finger marked in.

86

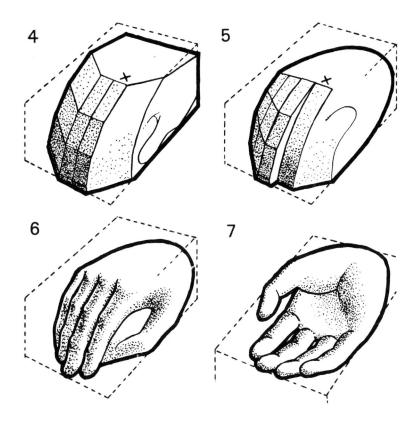

4   The wood on either side of the index and middle finger is cut back to the thumb and fourth finger.

5   The index finger is now cut back leaving the middle finger forward. Working in the opposite direction the back of the hand is rounded with a chisel or file and the fourth and fifth fingers and thumb marked.

6   A fine chisel cuts the surface divisions between the fingers, and between the index finger and thumb.

7   The hand is unscrewed from its block, turned over and from now on held in the hand. Paring from the finger-tips and wrist towards the centre, the palm and thumb are cleared. The finished hand is glued to its cardboard cylinder and the joint strengthened with tape.

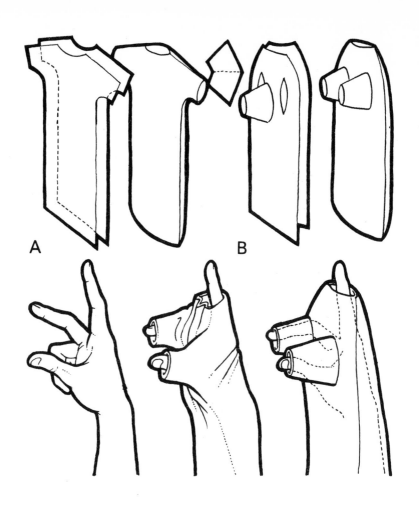

MAKING THE BODY

Here are two kinds of glove puppet body. Type *A*, often used in work with children, has an identical back and front with side-projecting arms. Type *B* has sleeves set in facing forwards. When in use the simpler pattern tends to gather between the arms, while the second pattern follows the shape of the operator's hand with less distortion. In either case wide sleeves tapering to the wrist conceal the different levels of thumb and third finger. The use of thick material gives an appearance of substance to a glove body, which with the addition of collar and cuffs, may also serve for clothing.

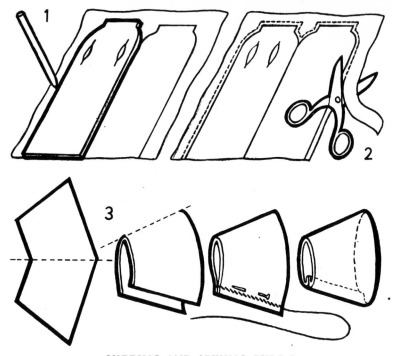

CUTTING AND SEWING TYPE B

1 A cardboard template is made from the scale pattern of type *B* body. This template is stencilled on to a piece of material wide enough to hold the front and back pieces side by side. The length of the glove body should extend to three quarters of the length of the operator's arm.

2 Allowing an extra width of 6 mm for sewing, cut round the outside of the pattern, leaving the joining of the two halves to be folded later. The spaces for the two sleeves are also cut out at this stage.

3 The sleeves are now cut from a stencilled line, folded, and sewn along the border.

4 Working from the inner side of the material of the body, the sleeves are pinned into place and sewn.

5 With the sleeves facing inwards, the body is folded across so that the front and back are in position.

6 The open side of the body and both sides at neck and shoulder

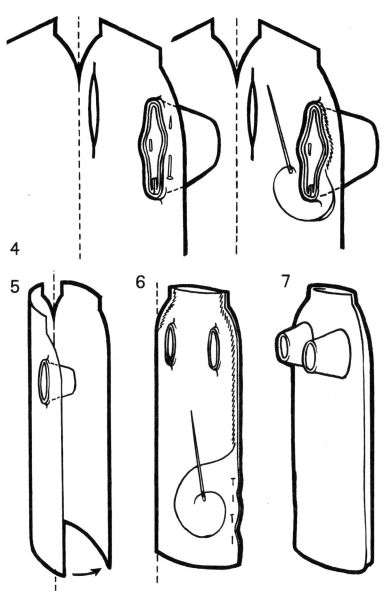

4

5 **6** **7**

are pinned into position and sewn.

7 The glove body is finally turned right side outwards, ready for the attachment of head, hands, and a hook to hang by.

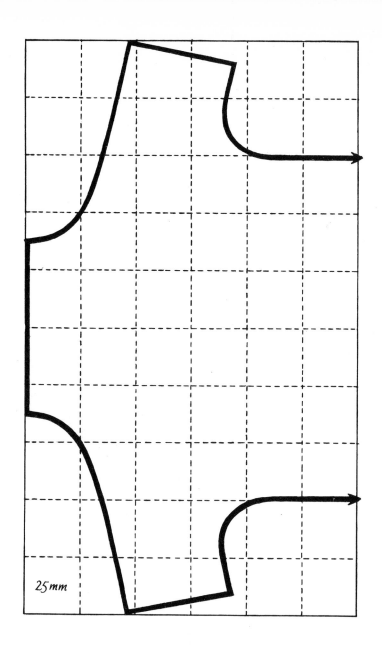

25mm

PATTERN FOR BODY TYPE A

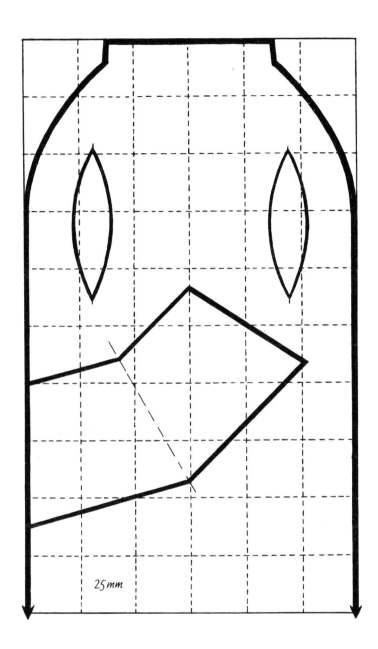

25mm

PATTERN FOR BODY TYPE B

THE HANGMAN AND THE DEVIL

94

CLOTHES

You will find in all puppets' clothing that outline is more important than detail, that colour and tone should stand out against background scenery, and that dress should never get in the way of manipulation.

For glove puppets the clothes and body may be of one piece. The addition of collar, cuffs and hat to the basic body pattern given earlier in this book may be quite sufficient as long as the material used has enough substance to keep its shape. The diagrams of the hangman and the Devil, on the facing page, show how little extra is needed in many cases.

For those who prefer removeable clothing over the basic body I have given patterns for Punch's coat and hat. I have used this basic wide sleeved dress for most of my puppets; but there are many ways of doing this, and a Punch and Judy show in today's costume will have problems of its own.

Almost any materials are suitable for puppets' clothes, but patterned material must be correct in scale. With so many cloth adhesives on the market there is no need for elaborate stitching except at stress points, and braid or nylon lace can be used to conceal hems in some cases. Cardboard stiffening should be used in making hats, and also for the humps of Punch and Scaramouch.

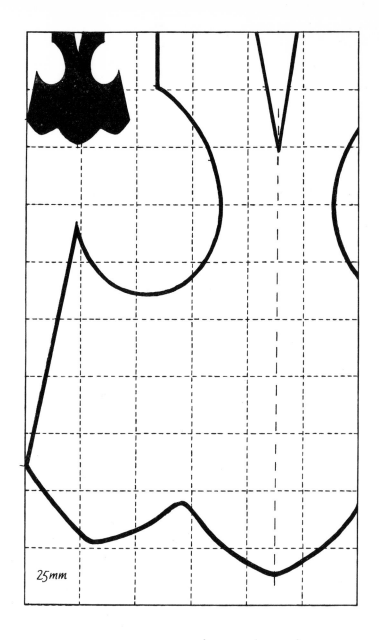

PATTERN FOR PUNCH'S COAT (FRONT)

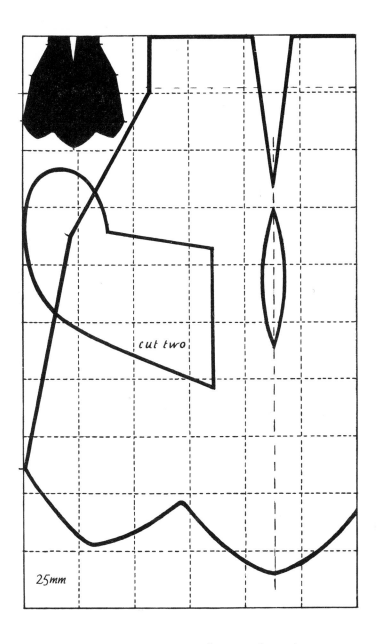

cut two

25mm

PATTERN FOR PUNCH'S COAT (BACK)

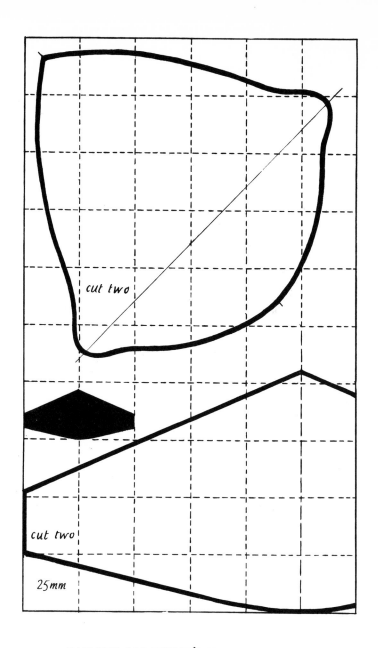

cut two

cut two

25mm

PATTERN FOR PUNCH'S HAT AND SLEEVES

98

TRICK PUPPETS

Several irregular puppets appear in the Punch and Judy show.
A Shows how legs are added to the basic glove. They may be made of felt, papier mâché, or wood, the upper half being of the same material as the body.
B Shows legs that are made in the same way as the arms, and manipulated by the operator's spare hand.
C Toby's head looks better if the wide neck fits over the body, not into it; with a cylinder inside for the operator's index finger.
D For the Courtier and Scaramouch a strong cardboard ring is fitted into the neck of the body. The Courtier's head is modelled on a free moving piece of broom handle, while Scaramouch's head has no neck. Those who wish to attempt the trick of removing the Courtier's hat will probably find that it can only be done by stringing.
E Polly can be modelled over a piece of broom handle built up from wire, papier mâché, and table tennis balls.
F The Baby is made from a papier mâché or wooden core extended with cardboard.

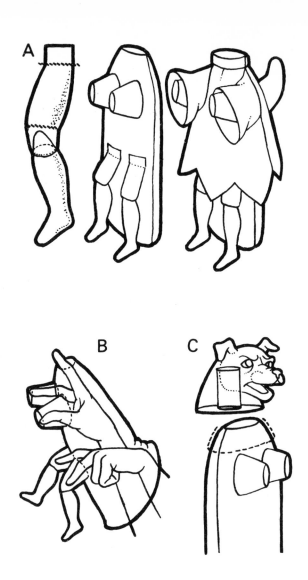

IRREGULAR PUPPETS—PUNCH AND TOBY

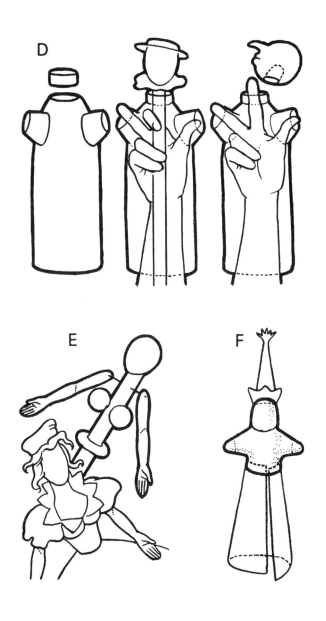

IRREGULAR PUPPETS—COURTIER, SCARAMOUCH,
POLLY AND BABY

ASSEMBLED BOOTH FROM BEHIND (WITHOUT CURTAINS)

THEATRES

The traditional Punch and Judy show was presented in a portable
booth. I have given here the basic design of such a one-man
theatre which can easily be enlarged to the scale of a group
production or permanent theatre, and altered for different
methods of manipulation.

In the first illustration puppets are held above the head in a
stage opening (proscenium) whose lower border is at the per-
former's eye level. This position presents puppets where they
can be seen over the heads of a standing audience. The inside of
the booth shows—(a) A curtain rail behind the upper border of
the proscenium; (b) A playboard where much of the action takes
place; (c) A shelf for properties when not in use; (d) A wire round
three sides of the booth on which puppets are hung and (e) A
canvas sling into which puppets are dropped when they have
played their part.

In a second less tiring method of manipulation the proscenium is lower, and the operator stands behind a semi-transparent screen resting his elbows on the properties' shelf. Light falls on the front of the screen, but the operator standing in the dark is invisible to the audience.

The framework of this portable booth is made from 4 jointed uprights of 25 × 25 mm hardwood, and cross battens of 25 × 13 mm fixed together by wing nuts and bolts. The top battens fit over dowel pegs, and planks for the playboard and properties' shelf fit on to metal angle brackets. A proscenium frame of hardboard or plywood is often painted with traditional fairground designs.

The covering material is in two parts: A canopy above, which fits over the top of the wooden uprights, and a surrounding curtain of striped or checked pattern below. The fringe round the playboard conceals an opening between the playboard and lower curtain which may be used by the puppets.

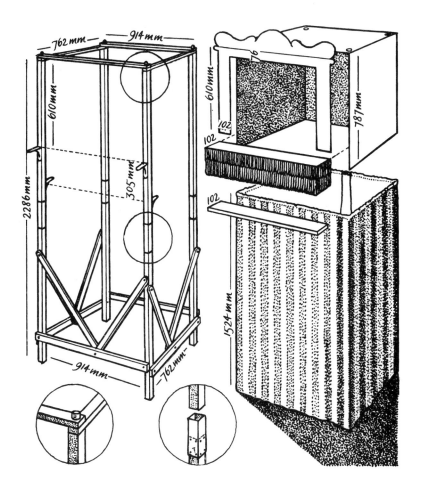

LIGHTING

Unlike the marionette theatre, the Punch and Judy show has
never been performed in an enclosed space of illusion, but right
in the lap of the audience. For this reason it has always shared the
light of its setting; daylight out of doors, or the artificial light of
a lighted room. If extra lighting is used its main purpose should
be to make the puppets visible, and one or two hundred watt
lamps directed from the front on to the playboard and puppets
should be enough for this purpose. There may be room inside the
booth for one further hanging lamp to light the backcloth, but
this will have little effect on the puppets themselves who are
nearly always at the front of the stage or on the playboard. For
those who feel that they must have colour changes and graded
lighting, I have given a list of suppliers at the end of this book,
who can provide catalogues and information.

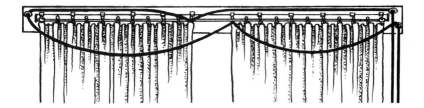

CURTAINS

Many Punch and Judy showmen have used no curtains, performing straight through without change of scene. However, curtains
do raise the curiosity of an audience before a show begins, and
may also close briefly before the prison scene to conceal changes
and prepare for difference in mood. Curtain rails can be fixed
permanently on to the back of the proscenium frame, and curtains
hooked on to their runners each time that the booth is re-
assembled.

PUNCH'S THEATRE

108

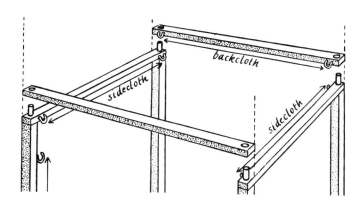

The early Piccini performance of Punch and Judy used back and side cloths of a formal Italian garden. Later shows often make use of an old English street scene. In either case scenery is painted on cloth or card and hung or pinned inside the cross battens at the top of the frame. If cloth is painted it must be prepared with a solution of glue size crystals melted in water to give it substance. Powder paint must also be mixed with glue size to prevent flaking. Acrylic paint tends to be more flexible.

When a transparent screen is used it becomes both screen and backcloth. The material can be dyed one general colour which does not effect its transparency, and the suggestion of a scene picked out in line heightened with white. Extra scenery (for example the prison window) may be hung from hooks on the inner surface of the front uprights of the frame, and swung into position when needed.

Properties in the Punch and Judy Show are the small articles handled, wielded, or thrown by the puppets during the course of the play.

Punch's stick must be big enough to be easily held, and a cooking spurtle is a good guide to size and thickness. Other sticks are mentioned in the drama; a bludgeon, the beggar's staff, and the Devil's stick. Sometimes Punch's stick is split at one end so that it makes a sharp crack when it strikes.

The bell can be an ordinary small table hand bell.

The gibbet can be as high as the stage opening. It is most safely fixed in position when it has a tapered end fitting into a socket in the playboard. The noose has a fixed knot and should hang at a convenient level for Jack Ketch's head. The rope hangs from a slot, and can be lifted out entirely when Ketch is put in his coffin.

The ladder has a few rungs near the top removed, so that it will stay in place leaning on the corner of the gibbet.

The coffin is an ordinary wooden box with handles added. Sometimes it is covered by a cloth pall which is easier to manage than a lid.

PRODUCTION

The Punch and Judy show is a succession of incidents rather than a subtle developing plot. It is wisest to accept the limitations of play and puppets, making the most of the qualities which they do have. Strong contrast in characterisation and great vitality of movement, colour and sound should be a constant stimulus to the audience. Here are some points which may be helpful in production.

PLANNING

It takes careful planning to fit all the parts of the Punch and Judy show together, particularly if you are working in a group. You will have to think ahead about the number of people who are to make and manipulate the puppets; the number of operators who may be inside the theatre at one time; the size of the theatre; the number of puppets in the cast and their size and proportions; the age group of the audience you expect to entertain; the extent of audience participation suitable; and whether the showman or manipulators are to appear as well as the puppets. With these points settled, the cast has the security of a basis on which to improvise, and may make use of happy accidents as they occur.

Rehearsals are most successful when they develop in stages, with plenty of opportunity for alterations and exchange of ideas.

1   As soon as the outline of the story as a whole is understood, each puppet should be tried out in free play before a mirror. In the same way that a child gives a toy a life of its own, the manipulator creates a personality for his puppet, until it acts instinctively in any situation.

2   For first rehearsals of puppets together, the manipulators can sit in chairs. It is important here not just to repeat a set script, but to act the *situations* from which words and movement naturally arise. Where puppetry is used as a means of expression for educational or therapeutic purposes this is essential.

3   Scene by scene rehearsals may begin in the theatre itself, working out immediate problems of grouping, passing, holding of properties, exit and entry. The placing of each of Punch's encounters should vary, and if there is more than one manipulator Punch need not be kept to one side of the stage only. Puppets with legs should be given opportunities to use them, and to sit on the edge of the playboard. In a one-man show Punch remains for most of the time on the manipulator's right hand, but the changing of the puppets on the left needs practice; each puppet in turn is shaken off into the canvas sling below leaving the left hand free to plunge into the next puppet hanging ready in position on the wire like a surgeon's glove.

4   As soon as the technical problems of staging are under control and all the scenes are set the show is ready for performance as a continuous whole, with music, sound effects and lighting. An observer in front of the theatre is in the best position to advise where contrasts may be brought out, and the action speeded up.

BUSINESS

This is the term given to what puppets do in addition to just speaking their parts; and thinking of ways for puppets to use their hands and feet, and handle properties, gives great scope for invention. A certain amount of business is described in the script, but here are some ideas from other Punch and Judy shows.

Punch and Judy play ball by throwing the baby back and forwards to each other; Punch, sitting on the playboard, beats time and crosses and uncrosses his legs during his songs; Properties are deliberately dropped from the playboard, and the audience appealed to by the puppets to hand them up again; Punch makes a count of the corpses at the end of the show and is confused by one survivor who pretends to be dead but keeps on re-appearing; a struggle takes place to fit Jack Ketch into the coffin which is too small for him; and always successful, Punch's enemies enter unseen by Punch whose back is turned, but fully visible to the audience.

MUSIC

Music has always been associated with Punch and Judy shows. Early performances were announced by a trumpet, and in the Victorian age the collector in front of the booth played on pan-pipes and beat a drum. There are plenty of popular songs to choose from today for Punch to sing, and also traditional folk airs for those who prefer them. Some showmen use recorded music although this allows no flexibility of timing, and full orchestral music is wrong in scale for small puppets. When no live instrumentalists are available, I would still prefer the directness of music made through comb and paper.

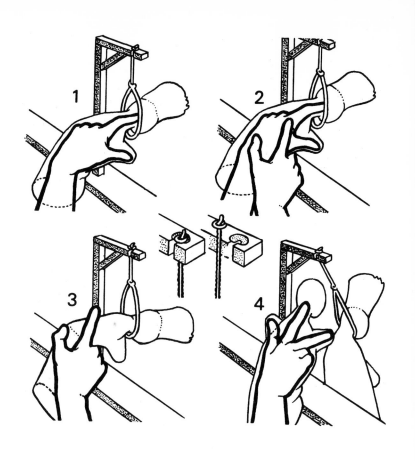

The handling of glove puppets presents few problems except in the gallows scene, or to a single showman when the script asks for more than two puppets on stage at one time.

In the diagram on the facing page .

1 Jack Ketch on the operator's left hand puts his head in the noose.

2 Punch on the operator's right grips him round the waist.

3 The left hand is withdrawn leaving Punch holding the empty glove.

4 Punch swings Jack Ketch in his noose over the playboard to hang in front of it.

By this same method the scene of Punch's arrest by three other puppets is carried out. While appearing to struggle, the Constable can hold Punch in his arms with the Officer pinned in a corner, leaving the operator's other hand free to fetch Jack Ketch.

In the prison scene Punch can be hung by his nose between the bars, leaving both of the operator's hands free to set up the gallows and bring in the coffin carriers.

MAKING THE SWAZZLE

SPEECH

Early Punch showmen spoke Punch's voice through a 'swazzle', an instrument held in the mouth which worked like the reed of a wind instrument. The swazzle produced a shrill, carrying sound, good for attracting an audience, but not always easy to understand. However the showman's assistant in front of the booth might repeat and interpret Punch's most entertaining remarks to the audience.

If you want to use a swazzle today you will need two pieces of thin metal (pewter or silver) of size 38 × 16 mm. These are bent into a curve, turned to face each other, and placed on either side of a 6 length of tape which is bound tightly round the outside of the two plates, and sewn in position. The swazzle is dipped in water before use and placed between the lips above the tongue. Speaking through the swazzle and alternating with normal speech takes practice but is well worth trying.

Other voices in the Punch and Judy show are spoken naturally although varied in accent and pitch and Judy speaks in falsetto.

The use of tape recorded dialogues, convenient in large string puppet productions, leaves no opportunity for impromptu speech and is inexcusable here. The whole expressive value of the glove puppet lies in its directness of control, which allows an immediate relationship between the thought, speech and movement of one actor-manipulator.

LIST OF SUPPLIERS

Materials and equipment are obtainable from the following
departments of stores and specialised shops

ARTS AND CRAFTS
Poster paint, powder paint, acrylic paint and oil paint for
puppets and scenery—White paste for *papier mâché*—Glue for
wood, cloth and cardboard—Craft knives—Modelling clay for
papier mâché pulp—Plasticine for modelling heads and to aid in
casting—paper of all kinds for plans and sketches—Sugar
paper for laminated *papier mâché*—Cardboard for properties
and hays—Paint brushes—Spirit varnish for sealing *papier
mâché*—Hardsetting modelling substances—Sheet pewter for
swazzle—Gold fringe for theatre—Braid and tassels for
costume

PAINTERS AND DECORATORS
Ceiling whiting powder—Cold water paste for *papier mâché*
Glue crystals for laminated *papier mâché* and for preparing
cloth for scene-painting

CARPENTER'S TOOL AND HARDWARE
Wire of all thicknesses for framework of *papier mâché* hands,
for framework of properties and for hanging rail inside
booth—Broomhandles for courtiers neck and supports for

Pretty Polly and Toby—Chisels, mallets, saws, planes, files and drills for making wooden puppets—Table vices Wing-nuts and bolts for portable theatres

CHEMISTS AND DRUGSTORES
Paper handkerchiefs and paper towelling for *papier mâché* Plaster of Paris for making moulds—Vaseline for greasing moulds—Roller bandaging for building cores for direct modelling of *papier mâché*

MODEL KIT SHOPS
Wood glues—Plastic wood for lining moulds—Plywood for Hector the Horse

STATIONERS
Office glue for laminated *papier mâché*

TIMBER MERCHANTS AND LUMBER YARDS
Lime or fruit wood for puppet heads and hands

WOOLWORTHS AND U.S. 5 AND 10C STORES
Cup hooks for hanging puppets—Electric fittings—Curtain rails, hooks and fixtures for theatre curtains

UPHOLSTERERS
Material for booth sides and canopy and curtains—Remnants for puppets' clothing

USEFUL WASTE MATERIAL
Remnants of fur and lambswool for puppets' hair—Fabric remnants for puppets' clothing—Used blankets for puppets' bodies—Newspaper for *papier mâché* pulp—Used tennis balls for cores of puppet heads—Used sheets for strip binding cores of puppet heads

For wholesale ordering of materials the catalogues of the following suppliers will be found useful:

GREAT BRITAIN
Dryad Handicrafts Ltd, Northgates, Leicester.
Nottingham Handicrafts Co., Helton Road, West Bridgeford, Nottingham.

Atlas Handicrafts, High Street, Manchester 4
Reeves & Sons Ltd, Lincoln Road, Enfield, Middlesex.
George Rowney & Co. Ltd, 10 Percy Street, London, w.1.
Margros Ltd, Monument House, Monument Way West,
Woking, Surrey (for *Multiples 100* modelling material).

USA
Dick Blick Co, Box 1267, Galesburg, Illinois 61401
Triarco Arts and Crafts, Dept. 4410, Box 106, Northfield,
Illinois 60093
J L Hamett Co, 290 Main Street, Cambridge, Massachussets.
Bergen Arts and Crafts, Box 689 SA, Salem,
Massachussets 01970
Arthur Brown & Brothers, 2 West 46th Street,
New York, N.Y. 10036
New York Central Supply Co., 62 Third Avenue,
New York, N.Y.
Creative Hands Co. 4146 Library Road, Pittsburgh,
Pennsylvania 15234

For stage lighting equipment catalogues can be ordered from:

GREAT BRITAIN
Strand Electric & Engineering Co. Ltd, 29 King Street,
London w.c.2.
W J Furse & Co. Ltd, 9 Cartaret Street, London, s.w.1.

USA
American Stage Lighting Co., 1331C North Avenue,
New Rochelle, N.Y. 10801
Capitol Stage Lighting Co., 509 West 56th Street, New York,
N.Y. 10019
Times Square Stage Lighting, 318 West 47th Street,
New York, N.Y. 10036

BIBLIOGRAPHY

Punch and Judy edited by John Collier from the performance of Puccini. Illustrated by George Cruikshank   Prowett Pall Mall London 1828

London Labour and the London Poor Henry Mayhew, Volume III pp. 43-60   Griffin Bohn & Co Stationer's Hall Court London 1861

How to do Punch and Judy Sidney de Hempsey   Max Andrews London 1939

Mr Punch Philip John Stead   Evans Brothers Ltd London 1950

The History of the English Puppet Theatre George Speaight George Harrap & Co Ltd High Holborn London 1955

NOTE FOR AMERICAN READERS

Throughout read

$\frac{1}{4}$ in. *for* 6 mm	4 in. *for* 102 mm
$\frac{1}{2}$ in. *for* 13 mm	18 in. *for* 460 mm
$\frac{3}{8}$ in. *for* 10 mm	2 ft *for* 610 mm
$\frac{5}{8}$ in *for* 16 mm	2ft 6in. *for* 762 mm
$\frac{3}{4}$ in. *for* 20 mm	2ft 7in. *for* 787 mm
1 in. *for* 25 mm	3 ft *for* 914 mm
$2\frac{1}{2}$ in. *for* 65 mm	5 ft *for* 1524 mm
3 in *for* 80 mm	7ft 6in. *for* 2286 mm